SU DOKU

100 FUN NUMBER PUZZLES

Compi...
Kjartan Poskitt &
Illustrated by ...

SCHOLASTIC INC.

New York   Toronto   London   Auckland   Sydney
Mexico City   New Delhi   Hong Kong   Buenos Aires

No part of this work may be reproduced, stored in a retrieval system, or transmitted in any form or by any means, electronic, mechanical, photocopying, recording, or otherwise, without written permission of the publisher. For information regarding permission, write to Scholastic Ltd., Euston House, 24 Eversholt Street, London NW1 1DB, United Kingdom.

ISBN 0-439-84570-X

All rights reserved. Published by Scholastic Inc., 557 Broadway, New York, NY 10012, by arrangement with Scholastic Ltd.

SCHOLASTIC, APPLE PAPERBACKS, and associated logos are trademarks and/or registered trademarks of Scholastic Inc.

12 11 10 9   6 7 8 9 10 / 0

Printed in the U.S.A.   40
First Scholastic U.S.A. printing, November 2005

CONTENTS

SUGGESTION! Use a pencil to complete the puzzles, so if you make a mistake, you can erase it and start again! As the puzzles get tougher, use two different-colored pencils. Use red to mark in numbers you are absolutely sure about. Then if you need to guess, start using black and keep using it. If your guess proves wrong, erase all the black numbers and guess again.

In the beginning . . .

City: Chicago, Illinois
Place: The Municipal Park
Date: October 2, 1928

One evening Blade Bolton and his six shady associates were sitting in the park gloomily staring at the late edition of the newspaper. They had been reading a story of seven men who had attempted a bank raid disguised with paper bags over their heads.

"Don't blame me," muttered Porky Bolton feebly. "I was only told to get the bags. Nobody mentioned cutting eyeholes in them."

"Why did they have to be old doughnut bags?" snapped Half-Smile Hickock, scraping a bit of old jam out of his hair.

"Don't be ungrateful," said Porky. "I had to empty every one of those bags myself just so you guys could have disguises. You don't think I enjoyed it, do you?"

"Just seven bags?" sneered Half-Smile. "The way you eat, I bet you didn't have time to enjoy it."

Things were about to get nasty. Already Porky was reaching for the sharpened dessert fork he kept under his hat, while Half-Smile was pulling his side-shooter from his side pocket.

"Cool it, guys," said Blade, trying to calm them down. "The main thing is that we got away."

"Only because everybody was too busy laughing to catch us," moaned the Weasel, a little man peering out from under a big hat. He was still trying to lick the sugar out of his nose.

"Whatever," said Blade. "For now we just stay quiet. Keep our heads down, and nobody will know it's us. Now let's read about something else." For a moment they all fell silent.

"What's that?" blurted Chainsaw Charlie, pointing to a strange square shape on page 27.

"It's a crossword, stupid," sneered the Weasel. "You never seen a crossword before?"

"I ain't never seen one," said Chainsaw, "but if you call me stupid again, you're gonna hear plenty of *cross* words . . ."

But the others were all ignoring him, their eyes glued to the square shape where the daily flower-arranging tips were supposed to be.

"I thought a crossword had words you had to write in," said the Weasel. "So how come this one only has a few numbers?"

Just then a sharp click of high heels made its way down the path towards them, bringing with it a waft of perfume. Immediately the seven men all sat up, straightened their ties and tried to look intelligent.

"I see you guys found the Su Doku," said Dolly

Snowlips, peering over the top of the newspaper. "So how you getting along?"

"Sue who?" replied Chainsaw Charlie.

"We're doing the crossword," explained Blade, "just like all the smart folks do."

"Smart folks, eh?" murmured Dolly. "So you're not the sort of folks that run around banks with doughnut bags over their eyes then?"

"NO!" they all shouted together slightly too loudly.

Dolly Snowlips raised an eyebrow and the very last corner of her mouth turned upwards in a smirk. "So this crossword that you smart folks are doing, I see it doesn't have clues."

"Nah! Clues is just for beginners," said Blade. "We don't need no clues. We're getting along fine. We reckon the middle line down is 'custard.' Ain't that right, guys?"

The others all nodded, but Dolly wasn't fooled.

"And so how are you gonna spell that?" asked Dolly. "Seeing as how there's a 3 and an 8 in the middle."

"C-U-S-3-T-8-A-R-D" said Blade, writing the letters in with his pen. "It's the new way of spelling. It's simple for us smart guys — you just put your age in the middle."

"Guess you'd be putting a pretty big number in any word you wrote, Dolly," said Half-Smile Hickock.

The other men all snickered, but then stopped dead. They realized they had just made a dreadful mistake. A chill breeze of fear whistled down through the park. Birds stopped tweeting, flowers stopped blooming, and overhead every cloud immediately went black. Even the water flying out of the fountain turned around and shot back into the nozzles and hid in the pipes until it was safe to come out again.

"Funny you should mention numbers, pretty boy." Dolly spoke quietly but her voice sounded like an ice skate being pushed sideways across a steel plate. "Because that's what this puzzle is all about. They print the answer in the night edition, so that's how long you've got to solve it."

"But, but . . ." Blade tried to say something but he couldn't.

"Oh, come on," said Dolly. "It's simple for you smart guys, you just said so yourself. I'll see you tonight, ten o'clock, at Lou's Diner, so make sure you bring the completed puzzle. And if you don't, I'll be calling Lieutenant Ptchowsky about who I saw dumping seven doughnut bags in the bin a moment ago."

A simple start to Su Doku

So what is this mysterious number puzzle that Blade and the gang have to complete? If you haven't seen a Su Doku before, it's a grid of squares that you have to fill in with numbers. A normal 9x9 Su Doku grid contains 81 squares. But before we move on to those, let's start with a 4x4 grid. You'll see that it is made up of 4 blocks, each containing 4 squares.

RULES:

Each of the numbers 1,2,3 and 4 must appear once and once only in . . .
- each row
- each column
- each 2x2 block.

NOTE: "Columns" go up and down. "Rows" go across. In Su Doku puzzles "blocks" are a little bunch of squares. In this simple puzzle, each block is 2x2 squares.

To solve this you could start looking at the top left 2x2 block. (We've shaded it to show which one we mean.)

You have to put a 3 in it somewhere, but where? It can't go in the two lower squares because there is already a 3 in that row. Therefore the only place left for a 3 to go is up in the top left-hand corner next to the 1.

Where does the 2 go in the top left block? It can't go on the left-hand side because there's already a 2 in that column, so it has to go in the bottom right-hand corner.

Where does the 4 go? There's only one empty place left, so the 4 must go there.

3	1		
4	2		3
2			
		4	

The top left 2x2 block is now finished!

To continue, you might look at the bottom left square — where does the 4 go? Then where does the 1 go . . . and so on.

Now that you've got the hang of it, you can fill in all the other squares yourself. The fun part is that you'll know if you've gotten it right, but just in case you need help, the answer is on page 128. Once you've done that you can give yourself a big KISS for being so clever. You have mastered the puzzle that is conquering the world.

You may feel that you've done enough. You've proved your point. Su Doku puzzles . . . no problem. You may now wish to focus your great brain on other trivial matters such as the origins of the universe or the alignment of complex infinities. But for the rest of us, we'll move up to tackle the standard sort of Su Doku puzzles.

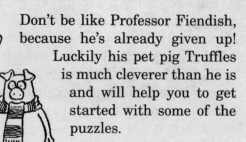

Don't be like Professor Fiendish, because he's already given up! Luckily his pet pig Truffles is much cleverer than he is and will help you to get started with some of the puzzles.

A Su Doku test drive

For normal Su Doku puzzles you have to put the numbers 1–9 once, and once only, in each row, column and 3x3 block.

WARNING – don't try to completely solve the puzzle on the next page because you can't! It doesn't give you enough clues. It's just a demonstration grid so that Thag, our Mystical Mathemagician, can explain a few of the basic solving tricks.

WE'RE GOING TO WORK OUT WHICH NUMBERS GO WHERE THE LETTERS ARE!

9	1	8	4	5	3	7	2	g
		2				e	3	f
		d		8				
7				6				
5							1	
h	5	b	3	c	2	4	7	8
			9			2	6	1
	8					5	9	a

Trick 1 PLUG THAT GAP. All you have to do is make sure every row, column and 3x3 block has 1–9 in it. Therefore the empty square labeled "a" at the bottom right MUST be 3 to complete that block. In the same way square g must be 6 to complete the top row.

Trick 2 THE MISSING LINKS. Look at the row starting with the letter h. There are three empty squares (h, b and c), and the missing numbers are 1, 6 and 9, so which way round do they go? The block containing square c already has a 9 in it, so the 9 cannot go in c. The column with h in it also has a 9, so it can't go there, so 9 must go in square b. As c is in a column with a 6 in it, it cannot be 6. Therefore h must be 6 and the only square left for the 1 is c.

Trick 3 TRIPLE-LINING. Here's something always worth looking out for. Look at the three columns on the left-hand side (ignore everything else for now). There's a 5 in the left-hand column and also a 5 in the middle column. You know the top 3x3 block needs a 5, so where's the only place it can go? That's right — in square d.

Trick 4 SECRET TRIPLE-LINING. Sometimes "triple-linings" are harder to spot. Look at the top three rows (ignore everything else for now). Using the "triple-lining" trick, you can see that there must be an 8 in either square e or f, but which is it? Don't give up yet! If you look down, you'll see the column with square f already has an 8 in it. Therefore the 8 has to be in square e.

Trick 5 NUMBER SWEEP. If you're lucky, you might suddenly find you can place all nine of one number in a grid! Here you can use triple-lining to place ALL the 8's, so why not give it a try?

Now you know enough basic tricks to attack our first set of puzzles, and as you go along, you'll even start to invent your own ideas. If worst comes to worst, we've got the Wise Mathematicians working out all the answers for you, starting on page 128. Off you go now, and GOOD LUCK!

DEAD SIMPLE PUZZLES

These puzzles give you something to do while waiting for a bus that's less embarrassing than aerobics.

1

	1		9				8	7
			2					6
					3	2	1	
		1		4	5			
		2	1		8	9		
			3	2		6		
	9	3	8					
7					1			
5	8				6		9	

Start by filling in all the number 1's and then all the number 9's. How satisfying!

TRUFFLES' TIPS

15

	8		2		9	6		
						9		1
1	9	6		8				
		4	6		2		5	
				9				
	2		1		5	8		
				3		5	1	4
3		7						
		1	5		8		6	

Where do all the 8's go?

TRUFFLES' TIPS

3

		1				4	7	9
4			7		2		6	
					5	8		
8			1					
	4		8		3		9	
					4			2
		9	3					
	7		2		1			8
6	2	3				9		

Where will 2 go in the top row?

	4	3		6				1
						7		4
		6	4			2		
	5		8					9
	2		1		4		7	
4					9		3	
		4			3	9		
2		1						
8				2		6	4	

Put all the 4's in. Where does 6 go in the second row?

TRUFFLES' TIPS

5

8					4	2	7	3
9						8		
		4	7				1	
	7		5			3	6	
				1				
	9	2			7		4	
	2				5	1		
		1						5
6	8	5	2					9

On the third row, what goes
in the last square on the right
(two places under the 3)?

TRUFFLES' TIPS

19

1				9	2			4
	3							5
	2			4			8	
	4		9	7		2		
	8						6	
		6		8	3		1	
	6			5			9	
5							4	
7			1	2				6

		4	6		8			
	6					7	3	
9	1				5	6		
6		1	8				7	
				4				
	2				7	9		5
		2	1				4	7
	4	6					8	
			7		4	5		

			5				1	
	8	3			1	5	4	
				9		7		
1				8	4			
2			1		5			9
			7	6				1
		9		5				
	3	5	2			8	6	
	7				6			

	4	2	8	1				
				6				
	5			9	4			3
	7						3	1
	3	8				5	9	
6	9						4	
4			3	2			5	
				4				
			8	9	6	2		

The middle block might be empty – but can you see where the 9 should go?

			3	7		1		
	9				8			
4		2		5	1	7		6
					7		4	
9								3
	8		4					
5		8	1	4		3		9
			6				2	
		1		9	5			

4						3		
	9				2			6
6	5				1		2	
7		6			8			
9		4				5		2
			4			1		7
	3		9				4	5
2			5				3	
		5						1

1			8		3			9
	3			9			7	
7	9						4	2
		1	6		9	7		
		9	4		5	2		
4	6						8	5
	2			4			6	
9			5		8			3

		5				3		
					9			
4	2			6		1		5
7		6		4	8			3
		8				9		
9			2	1		5		8
6		3		5			7	1
			4					
		2				8		

	3	4	6		8	7	9	
		8				3		
5	7						4	6
			1	3	9			
				8				
			4	2	5			
8	4						7	3
		7				2		
	9	5	2		7	6	8	

This one has TWO completely empty blocks! Leave these
until you have filled in all the other squares.
Then see what number goes in the top right
corner of the left-hand empty block (two
places below the 8). Next see what goes in
the middle of the top of the right-hand
block (immediately below the 4)...

TRUFFLES' TIPS

7					9		1	8
		9	2					
					8	3	9	
		1		8	6	7	2	
				2				
	9	6	7	1		5		
	4	2	6					
					4	6		
8	6		3					5

5	3			9			8	
6		2			7			
			5			7		3
8		6						1
		5				4		
3						8		2
9		1			2			
			4			5		7
	4			8			6	9

			3		6			
	7		4		9		8	
	3	6				2	4	
		9	2		5	8		
8								3
		5	8		4	7		
	8	1				6	5	
	2		9		8		1	
			1		2			

		2	4			7		6
						5		
			6	7			8	3
4	6		8	2				1
9				1	6		5	8
2	9		7	3				
		1						
5		8			2	9		

3			2		1			9
	4		7		9		3	
	6						5	
		2	1		6	8		
	8						4	
		4	9		2	6		
	7						6	
	9		6		3		2	
6			8		7			4

	4			6				
3				1	2	7	5	
		8		5	1	6	7	
		6	7		8	3		
	2	7	3	4		9		
	7	4	9	8				6
				7			2	

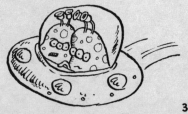

		1						
8		5	9		7	2		
		7		6	8			
9	3	2		4				
			3		1			
				9		4	5	3
			7	2		1		
		8	6		9	7		4
						3		

							4	
	8	1		3	7			5
			2	1	4			
	1			4		3	2	8
3	6	7		9			5	
			4	8	9			
1			6	2		4	9	
	3							

Before you do anything else here, can you see where the 2 must go in the central block? If you check the rows and columns, it seems there are two possible places on the right-hand side. But if you put 2 in the middle-right square of the central block, it's impossible to put a 2 in the left-hand block (the one with 3,6,7 along the bottom). Therefore the 2 has to be in the bottom-right square of the central block!

TRUFFLES' TIPS

23

5		4	8		6			
		9			4		2	
		7		1				5
	9				2			1
		5				2		
6			3				4	
9				2		3		
	5		7			1		
			4		3	7		6

4	5		8		7			
1	2		5					8
	6	9						
6	1			8				
			4		3			
				2			4	7
						7	5	
7					6		2	9
			2		1		3	4

9			2	8				7
	1					5	6	
6				9			3	
4	9							
7		3				8		1
							7	2
	4			7				3
	6	2					9	
1				4	9			5

		6				1		
	3			4			8	
5	9						3	2
		3	5		6	7		
8								3
		2	8		4	6		
2	8						5	7
	4			9			6	
		1				2		

	3					7		
1	4	2						9
6	8			4		2		
			9		8			
8			2		5			4
			4		7			
		6		9			7	8
7						6	1	5
		1					3	

1		4	7		8			9
		3	6					
	5				2			
4					7		9	
6	9						5	1
	7		8					2
			5				4	
					6	1		
3			2		4	9		7

				8		2	6	
2				9	1	4		
	1		3		5			
						9	8	6
5								4
4	3	9						
			8		7		9	
		3	5	1				7
	5	7		3				

		2		7	1		8	
			6				5	
					5		3	
5		6	3			1		9
		1				2		
9		8			4	3		5
	6		4					
	8				3			
	4		7	1		6		

DEVIOUS PUZZLES

These puzzles are about right for a short train journey.

Trick 6 LIL's LAST CHANCE

Now that the puzzles are getting slightly harder, it's time to call in a bit of help from some of our friends. When Riverboat Lil isn't earning an honest living at The Last Chance Saloon, she plays Su Dokus and here's one of her favorite tricks.

Look in the middle 3x3 block at the top of this grid. Where does the 7 go?

(Try to work it out before reading on!)

		2	4					6
3		8	6	2			5	4
	1			9		3		
		4	5				9	2
5					1			

As there are no other 7's in view, it might seem impossible to tell, but the way to do it is to check each empty square and see what could go in.

If you check the square to the right of the 2, the number that goes in it can't be 2,4,6 or 9 as they are in the same block. It can't be 3, 8 or 5 as they are in the same row, and it can't be 1 as it is in the same column. So the last chance you've got . . . is 7!

YOU SHOULD ALSO BE ABLE TO WORK OUT WHERE ALL THE OTHER NUMBERS GO IN THE TOP THREE BLOCKS.

WELL, SHOOT MA BOOT!

31

3	4		8			7		
	9	7		5		3		
	1		6			2		
							7	1
			1		9			
7	3							
		6			5		9	
		5		4		1	3	
		3			8		2	4

	6		9		5		1	
	3			7			9	
4	9						6	3
		6	4		3	5		
		2	5		9	8		
6	7						5	1
	8			5			7	
	2		7		1		8	

	1		2					
6				9		1		5
	3				4	9	7	
	8				1	4		
	4						6	
		7	9				2	
	2	4	1				5	
8		3		7				6
					5		8	

Look at the top right block and put
in the 2 and the 6, then the 8.

4								5
		5	4		7	9		
1	7						6	2
			1	2	8			
	8						2	
			6	5	3			
5	3						8	6
		8	7		6	2		
6								7

			4		8			
7	1		9				5	
8		5					3	
		3	8					
1		9				3		7
					7	9		
	9					2		1
	6				1		7	8
			2		6			

8			1	2	5	3	9	
				4				
	7	1				5		
		7		5				4
2				9		6		
		3				1	2	
				8				
	8	4	9	6	2			5

Quickly – where does the 7 go in the top right block? (See where it might go in the top-middle block first!)

TRUFFLES' TIPS

			9		4			
6	5		1				2	
2						1	4	7
				4			9	8
	7						6	
4	3			9				
7	9	6						1
	2				5		8	4
			3		9			

2								4
		9	5		4	2		
6		3				1		8
			4	5	8			
				7				
			6	2	1			
7		8				4		9
		4	3		9	8		
1								6

	9						2	
7		1				3		
2			3	1	4		8	
3				2	6			4
8			4	5				3
	7		6	9	5			8
		5				1		6
	4						5	

Where does the 1 go on the
seventh row?

			3		8			
	3		9		6		7	
7		8				6		3
		6	2		5	1		
	2						5	
		9	6		7	3		
9		2				8		4
	7		8		1		9	
			4		9			

Put all the 7's in to start with!

1			5		6			4
		8				6		
6	9						1	8
		2	7		3	5		
		7	2		5	4		
3	1						9	5
		9				8		
7			3		9			6

4			2		6			3
6	9	2				8	5	7
		7	5		1	2		
5								4
		9	7		8	5		
3	5	4				6	2	8
1			6		4			5

	8		4					
						1		
3		1			5		9	8
	9	3	8	6		5	4	
				7				
	7	6		3	4	8	1	
6	2		9			7		5
		4						
					7		2	

44

1	6		7		4		9	8
	9	5				2	4	
		1	9		8	4		
	2						3	
		3	4		2	1		
	4	7				6	2	
3	8		2		6		7	4

		5	3	7		1		
			8	4				
6						5	7	
1	4	3	6					
		9				7		
					1	4	3	2
	8	4						5
				6	8			
		1		9	4	8		

		5						
		9		6	4	8		5
8		3			5			6
		8	3				9	
		6				1		
	7				1	2		
6			5			7		4
9		2	7	8		5		
						3		

		9						
	1			4	9	2	8	
	4				6			7
		7		1				5
		4	7		2	9		
1				3		7		
3			6				4	
	6	1	2	8			5	
						1		

		4				7		
	2			4			8	
9		1				5		4
		9	8		7	3		
	7						2	
		5	3		9	6		
4		8				2		5
	1			6			9	
		2				8		

2			8		5	1		
2	9						5	
8			1	3	6			
				4	8	6	9	
				5				
	1	4	9	6				
			3	2	7			6
	7						2	
		1	6		9			3

Filling in the sixth column (with the 5 on top) is your easiest start here. Begin by finding a place for the 1 in the central block.

1		9				5		
6				3		2		1
			1	7	9			
		8	9				2	
	4						1	
	9				4	7		
			7	8	5			
9		7		6				5
		6				3		4

							6	2
		6			2			
				6		9		1
	1		3	2		6	7	
2		5				4		9
	7	8		5	4		1	
5		9		7				
			2			1		
3	8							

				6		1		
	6			9	8	7		
2	4				5			6
7		9	4					
3								5
					3	8		9
9			8				3	1
		1	9	3			8	
		4		2				

9			6					4
		8		3			5	
	6	5	4			3		
4					7			
	8	7				6	3	
			3					9
		2			6	9	7	
	9			7		2		
7					1			3

	2	7				5	4	
			7		5			
3		1				2		8
			5		7			
4	3						1	5
			3		2			
5		4				1		3
			6		4			
	7	8				9	2	

		2					7	
7	1							9
9					8		5	6
	9		2		4			8
5								7
2			8		5		1	
4	2		1					5
3							6	2
	6					8		

You can easily find what number goes in the very bottom left-hand corner square! And then, if you think about it, you'll see what has to go in the very top right-corner square!

TRUFFLES' TIPS

4	5						9	1
		2			9			
7	3	9				8		
2	7		5				8	
				1				
	6				8		7	5
		3				7	5	2
			6			9		
9	2						3	6

		4	3					6
7			8	2			3	
8		9		1				
			6			8		
1		8				5		3
		3			8			
				6		2		9
	9			4	1			8
2					7	3		

	4		9	6				
	2					4	1	
					7	5	6	
		8	4			2		
4			8		5			6
		3			9	7		
	3	6	7					
	9	1					3	
				9	3		8	

					2		3	
6				4				2
	4	5			8	6		
4		1						
8		7	2		3	9		4
						3		5
		9	4			8	7	
5				3				9
	6		8					

			4			2		
	7		1	3				5
					9	3		
2			8			7		9
9	3						4	2
1		7			3			6
		5	9					
6				2	4		8	
		9			6			

DRASTIC PUZZLES

These puzzles are suitable for a long bath if nobody else is waiting to use the toilet.

Trick 7 THE GREAT RHUN'S INVISIBLE BLOCK

The Great Rhun of Jepatti was the richest man who ever lived. He possessed many extraordinary skills, including this trick for solving Su Dokus. So if you find you get stuck on the Drastic puzzles, he has graciously consented to give you a hand.

2	x	y						a
3	4	7						b
v	6	w		5				7
								1
								9
								8
					5			c
								d
								e

Where does the 5 go in the right-hand column? Although there are five empty squares, it can't go in c, d or e as that block already has a 5 in it. This leaves square a or b.

Now see where 5 could go in the top-left block. It cannot go in v or w because there is already a 5 in that row. Therefore 5 must go in x or y. We don't know which, but what we DO know is that if 5 goes in x or y then there can't be a 5 in square a. So we know square b has the 5.

If you've already been doing the earlier puzzles in this book, you will probably have developed some other clever tricks of your own. Now it's time to line them up in your head, sharpen your pencil and take a deep breath because we're about to unleash something really nasty on you . . .

Actually it's even nastier than the Great Rhun's pet Ghinji. It's the DRASTIC puzzles!

61

		7	3			8	5	
1		3	6		2		4	
	4							
8			7			6	2	
				6				
	1	6			9			5
							7	
	5		8		6	4		2
	9	4			7	3		

You can start by filling in the
seventh column (the one with the 8
on top). Begin by finding a place for
the 5 and the 2...

6			7		8			9
				1		8		
	3					5	6	
				4		9	8	5
	8						7	
9	7	3		5				
	9	4					1	
		6		7				
8			4		5			2

1	2		9	5	7			
	8			3	1			
5								2
		9					1	
			6		4			
	3					4		
2								4
			4	7			6	
			3	1	9		7	8

8		3				1		9
		9	5		8	7		
2								8
		5	3		1	6		
	1						3	
		4	2		6	5		
5								7
		7	1		2	4		
4		8				9		5

Where does 1 go in the bottom-left block? Next you can complete the third column (with 3 on top), then the seventh column (with 1 on top).

8			6		9			1
		4	2		8	9		
3								6
		9	7		6	4		
	4						2	
		5	8		1	7		
5								4
		8	9		2	6		
9			1		4			2

It's even more fun if you solve
Su Dokus with a friend! Each of
you will spot things that the
other has missed.

			7	2	4		6	
		8				2	9	
			5					3
			8				1	2
7	6						4	9
9	8				6			
3					8			
	4	9				7		
	5		2	4	1			

					9		2	
		3				5		7
	4	2	5					1
4						1	9	
	1		3		8		5	
	2	7						6
1					7	6	4	
9		4				2		
	7		4					

					7	6		9
			5		8		3	
	3	1						2
					5	1	6	4
	7						2	
1	5	6	3					
3						2	8	
	1		9		3			
8		5	2					

Do you see that the middle
column is empty? Don't panic – the
top number is obvious!

		6					7	
2	8						4	9
		3	5			2	8	
9				7	5		3	
				1				
	7		8	2				4
	6	1			2	4		
7	5						1	8
	3					6		

3		9	2		8	5		1
				5				
5	7						8	4
		4	5		7	8		
		6	3		9	1		
6	2						9	8
				6				
4		7	8		1	2		5

	3		2		4		7	
		5	7		9	4		
7								5
		3	4		2	5		
	8						3	
		2	6		7	8		
6								9
		8	9		3	7		
	5		1		6		8	

		9	1		5		7	
	3					2		1
5					3			
		3	7	9	6			
9								4
			3	4	8	7		
			6					7
2		5					8	
	8		2		1	9		

6	3			1		9	8	4
				9		3	7	
	1							
		5	3				1	
			8		2			
	8				7	2		
							9	
	9	7		3				
3	5	1		2			4	6

			8					2
9		5						
4			5	9			3	
	5	9		2	8			
3								1
			3	1		5	6	
	1			3	4			6
						7		9
2					1			

7				1			6	
5			7			3	9	
	6		9		2			
		4			5			
3	1						5	6
			6			8		
			2		1		4	
	5	2			4			3
	4			9				1

1	2		5					
			2	9			3	1
		5		7			2	
		9			2			
6		2				1		3
			3			7		
	1			4		6		
5	6			3	9			
					6		7	5

			5		4			9
1		7		6		8	5	
	3							
		6			5		9	2
	4						8	
5	1		4			7		
							1	
	8	3		5		6		7
7			2		8			

Put the 5, then the 4, then the 9 in the top-left block. Now you can complete the second row!

TRUFFLES' TIPS

	6		5			8	7	
		7		6		4		2
						3		
5	9	6	7				4	
				2				
	1				4	6	5	7
		4						
8		5		1		9		
	7	1			9		3	

5	1		2		7		9	6
	4						5	
		3				7		
		5	1		6	9		
	7						2	
		6	7		5	1		
		2				4		
	5						7	
8	3		9		4		1	2

4		6		1	9		2	
5	9	1			8			7
						4		
2				7				
			3		6			
				2				5
		5						
3			5			7	8	1
	1		4	3		2		6

			6		9	3	8	
				7			9	4
			2	4		7		
		6	9					7
	3						4	
2					5	1		
		4		8	7			
9	5			2				
	1	2	5		3			

Those two empty blocks look nasty! But look at the bottom-center block. What is the only number that will go in the top left-hand square? Now see what is the only number that will go in the square below it, and then finish the block. Now look at the bottom-right empty block. What is the only number that will go in the left-middle square (two places below the 1)?

TRUFFLES' TIPS

	1						2	
		7	6		2	8		
8		3				4		6
			1	4	6			
	9						1	
			5	7	9			
5		1				3		2
		6	4		7	5		
	4						6	

	9				6			4
6	3		4	8				
4					3			2
	7	3						
2		1				4		5
						9	7	
8			6					9
				7	4		1	6
7			1				3	

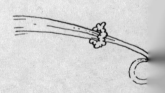

	7	8	6		1			
1	6				3	8		4
2				8				
	4			6				
		1				9		
				7			3	
				2				5
9		3	7				6	8
			8		9	2	4	

5		6	4					8
		2				1		
3			1				5	
	9		5		8		6	
7								5
	6		2		9		1	
	7				1			6
		8				9		
1					6	3		2

			9	7	1			
		2				1	8	
			5	8			6	
		4	7				1	5
8								2
9	6				8	4		
	4			2	7			
	2	6				3		
			6	1	4			

6		3						
		5					4	1
			8			3	9	
	9	4	2	5				8
1				9	3	2	5	
	7	6			2			
3	2					4		
						9		3

			7		6			
		4		5		8		
5	7						4	1
		1	6		4	3		
	9						2	
		8	2		5	1		
6	1						3	8
		2		7		6		
			5		8			

					8			5
	8	1					2	6
				3	6	4		7
5	7			4				
	2						4	
				7			9	8
7		5	2	9				
2	4					1	5	
1			5					

	4							5
6		7		5				
	9		6	1				
		4	1	6		5		
9	1						6	2
		2		7	3	4		
				8	1		5	
				9		2		8
2							9	

In the middle . . .

City: Chicago, Illinois
Place: The Municipal Park
Date: October 2, 1928
Time: 8:20 pm

Meanwhile Blade Bolton and his friends were still trying to finish the puzzle they started on page 7, but a sudden rainstorm had delayed them and almost destroyed their newspaper.

"We were doin' so well too!" moaned Porky Bolton. "We had loads of the numbers and letters in, even if it didn't make much sense. We could have finished it. Right, guys?"

The others all nodded together, which caused all the water to drip off their hats and hit the ground all at once with a musical splosh.

"So how are we gonna show Dolly that we got all the answers?"asked the Weasel.

"I guess we'll just have to write it all out again on a fresh piece of paper," said Blade, pulling out a piece of paper. "Somebody sharpen me a pencil and let's see what we can remember."

After some frantic arguing and scribbling, Blade looked at the results.

"There's still a lot more to go in," he muttered. "Anyone got any bright ideas what's next?"

Here's what they had gotten. Remember that they were using letters as well as numbers, but the rules are the same. Each of the letters and numbers in the grid has to appear once in each row, column and 3x3 block. Can you complete the puzzle?

				C	T	D	U	
D			A	U				
3				S				
A				3			T	
C		3		T		A		8
	U			8				C
				A				D
				R	8			S
	R	T	U	D				

DIABOLICAL PUZZLES

Finally, for these last puzzles there are no more tips or tricks we can give you. What you don't already know about Su Dokus, we can't tell you. You are on your own. We just feel that we

should warn you that these puzzles could take you a VERY long time...

LOOK! I'VE DONE IT!

6						3			1	
	7	2		5						
				6	2					4
						5		8		2
2	1								4	3
4		8		3						
7					5	6				
						1		6	2	
	3			2						8

At least this diabolical puzzle has an easy start! Where do all the 2's go? Where does 8 go on the seventh row? Where does 1 go in the top-center block? Then where do 1 and then 4 go in the central block? Now keep going...you can do it!

TRUFFLES' TIPS

2	9						8	3
			9		3			
5		3				2		6
		4	3		8	7		
	1						5	
		8	2		1	6		
1		5				9		4
			1		5			
4	3						1	2

5			1	3				
	2						1	
	9		6			5	7	
9	6	2	8					
			2		7			
					3	4	6	2
	3	1			8		4	
	7						8	
				7	5			6

	6	7					8	
			4	3				
3		9			6		1	
	4		3			2	7	
1								8
	3	6			1		4	
	9		2			1		6
				4	7			
	8					7	3	

	2	4	7					
6								5
			3	1	6	2		
5			2				3	
	1	6				4	2	
	4				1			7
		8	9	5	3			
2								9
					7	6	4	

4			9					
5	8						4	9
	2		4	8		6		
	3				9	4		
			6		5			
		8	2				9	
		5		6	3		8	
6	1						3	7
					4			2

6					3			5
9		3		8				
	5	1				6		
			4	3				7
		8	5		7	1		
4				6	8			
		7				9	8	
				7		4		2
8			3					6

3					2			6
		2			1	3		4
	4							
	9			5	3			
	1	4	9		8	5	3	
			7	1			8	
							6	
4		7	3			1		
5			6					8

7			1	9				
						2	1	
3	9			2	8			
			9	6	1			5
		8				3		
1			3	8	4			
			8	4			5	3
	5	7						
				1	7			4

The hardest Su Doku puzzle of all!

If you've got the kind of super-brain that enjoys diabolical Su Doku puzzles, there's one extra puzzle that you might like to hear about. As you know, while you've been working through the book, our expert team of Wise Mathematicians are racing ahead of you trying to get all the answers ready in case you need them.

NEARLY DONE!

HOW EXCITING!

IT'S EVEN MORE FUN THAN COUNTING TO A MILLION.

But along the way a rather scary question occurred to them. How many different Su Doku grids are there? In other words how many different ways can you put all the numbers 1–9 into a Su Doku grid so that they obey the rules? This turns out to be a really murderous piece of math, and since you deserve at least one clever chapter from this book, here it is. Don't worry if you don't understand it; it's just to give you an idea of what a really tough question this is!

As you know, the numbers 1–9 have to appear once and once only in every row, column and 3x3 block.

To start off we'll pretend that life is much simpler and that columns and 3x3 blocks don't matter. The only rule is that the numbers 1–9 have to appear once in every row. The first job is to see how many ways the numbers 1–9 could go into the top row, so we'll put the numbers in one at a time starting with the 1. Since the whole row is empty, the 1 has a choice of nine squares to go into.

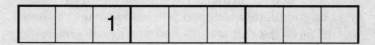

Now when we come to put the 2 in, we have a choice of eight empty squares . . .

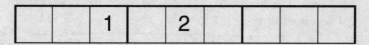

The total number of different ways we could put in the 1 and then the 2 is 9x8.

The 3 can now go in any of the seven empty squares and then the 4 can go in one of the six empty squares and so on. By the time you've put all nine numbers in, here's how they might appear:

If you've studied probability, you'll know that the total number of different ways the numbers could appear in the top row is written as 9! which is a quick way of writing $9 \times 8 \times 7 \times 6 \times 5 \times 4 \times 3 \times 2 \times 1 = 362{,}880$.

If we didn't care about numbers appearing only once in the columns and squares, then the second row would not be affected by the top row at all. Therefore there would be 9! ways of filling in the second row too. (One of those ways would be exactly the same as the top row but it wouldn't matter. In fact lots of the ways would have one or more numbers in the same place as the top row but that wouldn't matter either.) All the other rows would also be completely independent and so each of them would have the full selection of 9! ways of arranging the numbers. Therefore the total number of ways you could arrange the numbers in the nine rows = $(9!)^9$ = 9! x9! x9! x9! x9! x9! x9! x9! x9! = a very big number. (It's about 1 with 50 zeros after it, so it's a bit too boring to print here.)

IT SOUNDS REAL INTERESTING TO US!

Now suppose a number could only appear once in each row and only appear once in each column. As before, for the first row the numbers could appear in 9! different ways. When we come to put the first 1 in the second row, there is one place in which it can't appear.

3	7	1	5	2	9	6	4	8
		a						

Here number 1 can't appear in square a, so there are only eight possible squares left. Suppose it goes under the 4 . . .

3	7	1	5	2	9	6	4	8
				b			1	

Where can the number 2 go? It can't appear in the
square with a 1 in it, or the square marked b, so you
might think that the 2 only has seven squares to go
in. Unfortunately that is not always the case!

Just suppose the 1 had gone in here:

3	7	1	5	2	9	6	4	8
				1				

You'll see the 2 has eight squares it can go into.
Therefore the number of empty squares where the 2
can go depends on where the 1 goes. There's 8/9ths of
a chance there will be seven squares and a 1/9th
chance there will be eight squares. Already the math
is getting nasty, and so far we're only trying to get
two numbers onto the second line. After that we've
still got another 70 numbers to go into the grid, so
imagine how gross the math will be after that!

Now just suppose we managed to fill in the whole
grid so that the columns and rows were OK, and just
suppose we managed to cope with the math (dream
on). Here's how the first three rows might look:

3	7	1	5	2	9	6	4	8
7	5	4	1	6	8	3	2	9
6	9	2	8	5	4	7	1	3

So far so good, but don't forget that Su Doku doesn't allow any number to appear more than once in the same 3x3 block! Therefore the 7, 5 and 3 are all breaking the rules.

Amazingly some people have managed to battle through all this and work out that the number of ways you can put the numbers 1–9 into a proper Su Doku grid is = $9! \times 72^2 \times 2^7 \times 27,704,267,971 =$ 6,670,903,752,021,072,936,960.

Usually we'd try really, really hard to explain how everything works, but we're smart enough to know when we're beaten.

If we did try, we might manage to fathom what the $9! \times 72^2 \times 2^7$ in the sum is all about, but the really weird part is the number 27,704,267,971. This is a prime number (in other words it doesn't divide exactly by anything apart from 1 and itself), and where it crawled out from is a complete mystery. However plenty of clever people think it's right, so who are we to argue?

By the way if you've never seen prime numbers before, here's your chance. The first nine prime numbers are 2, 3, 5, 7, 11, 13, 17, 19, 23. The list of primes goes on forever, but just for fun we'll slap this set into a Su Doku and see how you get along. The rules are the same — each prime appears once and once only in each column, row and 3x3 block.

					17			3
3	7			5	2		11	17
23		17	11					
	23	11					2	
				11				
	13					11	23	
					3	2		
13	11		19	23			3	5
7			5					

Let's just see how the Wise Mathematicians are getting along with their careful calculation of the answers . . .

SOLUTIONS

Here are all the answers, which have been carefully worked out for you by our expert team of Wise Mathematicians. (And there's absolutely no truth in the rumors that they have been spying on the devious Mr. M who made up all the puzzles.)

First of all here's the solution to the 4x4 puzzle on page 10:

3	1	2	4
4	2	1	3
2	4	3	1
1	3	4	2

Dead Simple Solutions

1

2	1	5	9	6	4	3	8	7
8	3	9	2	1	7	4	5	6
6	4	7	5	8	3	2	1	9
9	7	1	6	4	5	8	2	3
3	6	2	1	7	8	9	4	5
4	5	8	3	2	9	6	7	1
1	9	3	8	5	2	7	6	4
7	2	6	4	9	1	5	3	8
5	8	4	7	3	6	1	9	2

2

5	8	3	2	1	9	6	4	7
4	7	2	3	5	6	9	8	1
1	9	6	7	8	4	3	2	5
8	3	4	6	7	2	1	5	9
6	1	5	8	9	3	4	7	2
7	2	9	1	4	5	8	3	6
2	6	8	9	3	7	5	1	4
3	5	7	4	6	1	2	9	8
9	4	1	5	2	8	7	6	3

3

2	5	1	6	3	8	4	7	9
4	9	8	7	1	2	5	6	3
3	6	7	9	4	5	8	2	1
8	3	2	1	6	9	7	5	4
7	4	5	8	2	3	1	9	6
9	1	6	5	7	4	3	8	2
1	8	9	3	5	6	2	4	7
5	7	4	2	9	1	6	3	8
6	2	3	4	8	7	9	1	5

4

9	4	3	7	6	2	5	8	1
5	1	2	3	9	8	7	6	4
7	8	6	4	1	5	2	9	3
1	5	7	8	3	6	4	2	9
3	2	9	1	5	4	8	7	6
4	6	8	2	7	9	1	3	5
6	7	4	5	8	3	9	1	2
2	9	1	6	4	7	3	5	8
8	3	5	9	2	1	6	4	7

5

8	1	6	9	5	4	2	7	3
9	3	7	1	2	6	8	5	4
2	5	4	7	8	3	9	1	6
4	7	8	5	9	2	3	6	1
5	6	3	4	1	8	7	9	2
1	9	2	3	6	7	5	4	8
3	2	9	6	4	5	1	8	7
7	4	1	8	3	9	6	2	5
6	8	5	2	7	1	4	3	9

6

1	5	8	3	9	2	6	7	4
4	3	7	8	6	1	9	2	5
6	2	9	7	4	5	3	8	1
3	4	1	9	7	6	2	5	8
9	8	5	2	1	4	7	6	3
2	7	6	5	8	3	4	1	9
8	6	3	4	5	7	1	9	2
5	1	2	6	3	9	8	4	7
7	9	4	1	2	8	5	3	6

7

2	3	4	6	7	8	1	5	9
8	6	5	2	1	9	7	3	4
9	1	7	4	3	5	6	2	8
6	5	1	8	9	2	4	7	3
3	7	9	5	4	1	8	6	2
4	2	8	3	6	7	9	1	5
5	9	2	1	8	6	3	4	7
7	4	6	9	5	3	2	8	1
1	8	3	7	2	4	5	9	6

8

7	6	4	5	2	3	9	1	8
9	8	3	6	7	1	5	4	2
5	2	1	4	9	8	7	3	6
1	5	6	9	8	4	2	7	3
2	4	7	1	3	5	6	8	9
3	9	8	7	6	2	4	5	1
6	1	9	8	5	7	3	2	4
4	3	5	2	1	9	8	6	7
8	7	2	3	4	6	1	9	5

9

3	4	2	8	1	7	9	6	5
9	8	1	5	6	3	4	7	2
7	5	6	2	9	4	1	8	3
2	7	4	9	5	6	8	3	1
1	3	8	4	7	2	5	9	6
6	9	5	1	3	8	2	4	7
4	6	9	3	2	1	7	5	8
8	2	7	6	4	5	3	1	9
5	1	3	7	8	9	6	2	4

10

8	5	6	3	7	4	1	9	2
1	9	7	2	6	8	4	3	5
4	3	2	9	5	1	7	8	6
6	1	3	5	2	7	9	4	8
9	7	4	8	1	6	2	5	3
2	8	5	4	3	9	6	1	7
5	6	8	1	4	2	3	7	9
7	4	9	6	8	3	5	2	1
3	2	1	7	9	5	8	6	4

11

4	7	2	8	6	5	3	1	9
3	9	1	7	4	2	8	5	6
6	5	8	3	9	1	7	2	4
7	2	6	1	5	8	4	9	3
9	1	4	6	7	3	5	8	2
5	8	3	4	2	9	1	6	7
1	3	7	9	8	6	2	4	5
2	4	9	5	1	7	6	3	8
8	6	5	2	3	4	9	7	1

12

1	4	2	8	7	3	6	5	9
5	3	6	2	9	4	8	7	1
7	9	8	1	5	6	3	4	2
2	5	1	6	8	9	7	3	4
3	8	4	7	1	2	5	9	6
6	7	9	4	3	5	2	1	8
4	6	3	9	2	7	1	8	5
8	2	5	3	4	1	9	6	7
9	1	7	5	6	8	4	2	3

13

8	7	5	1	2	4	3	9	6
3	6	1	5	8	9	7	2	4
4	2	9	7	6	3	1	8	5
7	5	6	9	4	8	2	1	3
2	1	8	6	3	5	9	4	7
9	3	4	2	1	7	5	6	8
6	9	3	8	5	2	4	7	1
5	8	7	4	9	1	6	3	2
1	4	2	3	7	6	8	5	9

14

1	3	4	6	5	8	7	9	2
2	6	8	9	7	4	3	1	5
5	7	9	3	1	2	8	4	6
7	5	6	1	3	9	4	2	8
4	2	1	7	8	6	5	3	9
9	8	3	4	2	5	1	6	7
8	4	2	5	6	1	9	7	3
6	1	7	8	9	3	2	5	4
3	9	5	2	4	7	6	8	1

15

7	3	4	5	6	9	2	1	8
1	8	9	2	3	7	4	5	6
6	2	5	1	4	8	3	9	7
4	5	1	9	8	6	7	2	3
3	7	8	4	2	5	9	6	1
2	9	6	7	1	3	5	8	4
5	4	2	6	7	1	8	3	9
9	1	3	8	5	4	6	7	2
8	6	7	3	9	2	1	4	5

16

5	3	7	2	9	1	6	8	4
6	8	2	3	4	7	1	9	5
4	1	9	5	6	8	7	2	3
8	2	6	7	5	4	9	3	1
1	9	5	8	2	3	4	7	6
3	7	4	9	1	6	8	5	2
9	5	1	6	7	2	3	4	8
2	6	8	4	3	9	5	1	7
7	4	3	1	8	5	2	6	9

17

4	9	8	3	2	6	1	7	5
5	7	2	4	1	9	3	8	6
1	3	6	5	8	7	2	4	9
3	1	9	2	7	5	8	6	4
8	4	7	6	9	1	5	2	3
2	6	5	8	3	4	7	9	1
9	8	1	7	4	3	6	5	2
6	2	3	9	5	8	4	1	7
7	5	4	1	6	2	9	3	8

18

3	8	2	4	5	1	7	9	6
6	7	9	2	8	3	5	1	4
1	5	4	9	6	7	2	8	3
4	6	5	8	2	9	3	7	1
8	1	3	5	7	4	6	2	9
9	2	7	3	1	6	4	5	8
2	9	6	7	3	8	1	4	5
7	4	1	6	9	5	8	3	2
5	3	8	1	4	2	9	6	7

19

3	5	7	2	6	1	4	8	9
8	4	1	7	5	9	2	3	6
2	6	9	4	3	8	7	5	1
7	3	2	1	4	6	8	9	5
9	8	6	3	7	5	1	4	2
5	1	4	9	8	2	6	7	3
1	7	3	5	2	4	9	6	8
4	9	8	6	1	3	5	2	7
6	2	5	8	9	7	3	1	4

20

7	8	2	5	3	9	4	6	1
5	4	1	8	6	7	2	9	3
3	6	9	4	1	2	7	5	8
9	3	8	2	5	1	6	7	4
4	5	6	7	9	8	3	1	2
1	2	7	3	4	6	9	8	5
2	7	4	9	8	5	1	3	6
8	1	3	6	7	4	5	2	9
6	9	5	1	2	3	8	4	7

21

6	2	1	4	5	3	9	7	8
8	4	5	9	1	7	2	3	6
3	9	7	2	6	8	5	4	1
9	3	2	5	4	6	8	1	7
5	8	4	3	7	1	6	9	2
7	1	6	8	9	2	4	5	3
4	6	3	7	2	5	1	8	9
1	5	8	6	3	9	7	2	4
2	7	9	1	8	4	3	6	5

22

2	9	3	5	6	8	7	4	1
4	8	1	9	3	7	2	6	5
6	7	5	2	1	4	8	3	9
5	1	9	7	4	6	3	2	8
8	4	2	3	5	1	9	7	6
3	6	7	8	9	2	1	5	4
7	2	6	4	8	9	5	1	3
1	5	8	6	2	3	4	9	7
9	3	4	1	7	5	6	8	2

23

5	2	4	8	3	6	9	1	7
1	3	9	5	7	4	6	2	8
8	6	7	2	1	9	4	3	5
3	9	8	6	4	2	5	7	1
7	4	5	9	8	1	2	6	3
6	1	2	3	5	7	8	4	9
9	7	6	1	2	5	3	8	4
4	5	3	7	6	8	1	9	2
2	8	1	4	9	3	7	5	6

24

4	5	3	8	6	7	9	1	2
1	2	7	5	9	4	3	6	8
8	6	9	1	3	2	4	7	5
6	1	4	7	8	5	2	9	3
9	7	2	4	1	3	5	8	6
3	8	5	6	2	9	1	4	7
2	3	6	9	4	8	7	5	1
7	4	1	3	5	6	8	2	9
5	9	8	2	7	1	6	3	4

25

9	3	5	2	8	6	4	1	7
2	1	8	7	3	4	5	6	9
6	7	4	5	9	1	2	3	8
4	9	1	8	2	7	3	5	6
7	2	3	9	6	5	8	4	1
8	5	6	4	1	3	9	7	2
5	4	9	6	7	2	1	8	3
3	6	2	1	5	8	7	9	4
1	8	7	3	4	9	6	2	5

26

4	2	6	9	8	3	1	7	5
1	3	7	2	4	5	9	8	6
5	9	8	6	1	7	4	3	2
9	1	3	5	2	6	7	4	8
8	6	4	1	7	9	5	2	3
7	5	2	8	3	4	6	1	9
2	8	9	4	6	1	3	5	7
3	4	5	7	9	2	8	6	1
6	7	1	3	5	8	2	9	4

27

9	3	5	6	8	2	7	4	1
1	4	2	7	5	3	8	6	9
6	8	7	1	4	9	2	5	3
5	6	4	9	1	8	3	2	7
8	7	3	2	6	5	1	9	4
2	1	9	4	3	7	5	8	6
3	2	6	5	9	1	4	7	8
7	9	8	3	2	4	6	1	5
4	5	1	8	7	6	9	3	2

28

1	6	4	7	3	8	5	2	9
9	2	3	6	1	5	8	7	4
8	5	7	9	4	2	3	1	6
4	3	2	1	5	7	6	9	8
6	9	8	4	2	3	7	5	1
5	7	1	8	6	9	4	3	2
7	8	6	5	9	1	2	4	3
2	4	9	3	7	6	1	8	5
3	1	5	2	8	4	9	6	7

29

3	9	5	7	8	4	2	6	1
2	7	8	6	9	1	4	3	5
6	1	4	3	2	5	8	7	9
7	2	1	4	5	3	9	8	6
5	8	6	9	7	2	3	1	4
4	3	9	1	6	8	7	5	2
1	6	2	8	4	7	5	9	3
8	4	3	5	1	9	6	2	7
9	5	7	2	3	6	1	4	8

30

3	5	2	9	7	1	4	8	6
8	9	4	6	3	2	7	5	1
6	1	7	8	4	5	9	3	2
5	2	6	3	8	7	1	4	9
4	3	1	5	9	6	2	7	8
9	7	8	1	2	4	3	6	5
1	6	3	4	5	9	8	2	7
7	8	9	2	6	3	5	1	4
2	4	5	7	1	8	6	9	3

Devious Solutions

31

3	4	2	8	9	1	7	6	5
6	9	7	2	5	4	3	1	8
5	1	8	6	3	7	2	4	9
8	6	9	5	2	3	4	7	1
2	5	4	1	7	9	6	8	3
7	3	1	4	8	6	9	5	2
4	2	6	3	1	5	8	9	7
9	8	5	7	4	2	1	3	6
1	7	3	9	6	8	5	2	4

32

2	6	7	9	3	5	4	1	8
8	3	1	6	7	4	2	9	5
4	9	5	1	2	8	7	6	3
9	1	6	4	8	3	5	2	7
3	5	8	2	6	7	1	4	9
7	4	2	5	1	9	8	3	6
6	7	9	8	4	2	3	5	1
1	8	4	3	5	6	9	7	2
5	2	3	7	9	1	6	8	4

33

4	1	9	2	5	7	6	3	8
6	7	2	8	9	3	1	4	5
5	3	8	6	1	4	9	7	2
2	8	5	7	6	1	4	9	3
9	4	1	5	3	2	8	6	7
3	6	7	9	4	8	5	2	1
7	2	4	1	8	6	3	5	9
8	5	3	4	7	9	2	1	6
1	9	6	3	2	5	7	8	4

34

4	6	9	3	1	2	8	7	5
8	2	5	4	6	7	9	1	3
1	7	3	8	9	5	4	6	2
7	5	4	1	2	8	6	3	9
3	8	6	9	7	4	5	2	1
2	9	1	6	5	3	7	4	8
5	3	7	2	4	9	1	8	6
9	1	8	7	3	6	2	5	4
6	4	2	5	8	1	3	9	7

35

9	3	6	4	5	8	7	1	2
7	1	2	9	6	3	8	5	4
8	4	5	7	1	2	6	3	9
6	7	3	8	2	9	1	4	5
1	2	9	6	4	5	3	8	7
4	5	8	1	3	7	9	2	6
3	9	7	5	8	4	2	6	1
2	6	4	3	9	1	5	7	8
5	8	1	2	7	6	4	9	3

36

8	4	6	1	2	5	3	9	7
5	3	2	7	4	9	8	1	6
9	7	1	6	3	8	5	4	2
3	1	7	2	5	6	9	8	4
4	6	9	8	1	7	2	5	3
2	5	8	4	9	3	6	7	1
6	9	3	5	7	4	1	2	8
7	2	5	3	8	1	4	6	9
1	8	4	9	6	2	7	3	5

37

3	1	7	9	2	4	8	5	6
6	5	4	1	7	8	3	2	9
2	8	9	5	3	6	1	4	7
5	6	1	2	4	3	7	9	8
9	7	2	8	5	1	4	6	3
4	3	8	6	9	7	2	1	5
7	9	6	4	8	2	5	3	1
1	2	3	7	6	5	9	8	4
8	4	5	3	1	9	6	7	2

38

2	5	7	1	8	6	3	9	4
8	1	9	5	3	4	2	6	7
6	4	3	7	9	2	1	5	8
3	7	6	4	5	8	9	2	1
4	2	1	9	7	3	6	8	5
9	8	5	6	2	1	7	4	3
7	3	8	2	6	5	4	1	9
5	6	4	3	1	9	8	7	2
1	9	2	8	4	7	5	3	6

39

4	9	3	5	8	7	6	2	1
7	8	1	9	6	2	3	4	5
2	5	6	3	1	4	9	8	7
3	1	7	8	2	6	5	9	4
5	6	4	7	3	9	8	1	2
8	2	9	4	5	1	7	6	3
1	7	2	6	9	5	4	3	8
9	3	5	2	4	8	1	7	6
6	4	8	1	7	3	2	5	9

40

5	6	1	3	7	8	4	2	9
2	3	4	9	1	6	5	7	8
7	9	8	5	4	2	6	1	3
3	4	6	2	9	5	1	8	7
8	2	7	1	3	4	9	5	6
1	5	9	6	8	7	3	4	2
9	1	2	7	5	3	8	6	4
4	7	3	8	6	1	2	9	5
6	8	5	4	2	9	7	3	1

41

1	2	3	5	8	6	9	7	4
4	7	8	9	3	1	6	5	2
6	9	5	4	7	2	3	1	8
9	6	2	7	4	3	5	8	1
5	4	1	6	9	8	2	3	7
8	3	7	2	1	5	4	6	9
3	1	6	8	2	4	7	9	5
2	5	9	1	6	7	8	4	3
7	8	4	3	5	9	1	2	6

42

4	8	5	2	7	6	1	9	3
7	1	3	9	8	5	4	6	2
6	9	2	4	1	3	8	5	7
8	4	7	5	6	1	2	3	9
5	6	1	3	2	9	7	8	4
2	3	9	7	4	8	5	1	6
3	5	4	1	9	7	6	2	8
9	7	6	8	5	2	3	4	1
1	2	8	6	3	4	9	7	5

43

9	8	7	4	1	3	2	5	6
4	5	2	6	9	8	1	7	3
3	6	1	7	2	5	4	9	8
1	9	3	8	6	2	5	4	7
8	4	5	1	7	9	3	6	2
2	7	6	5	3	4	8	1	9
6	2	8	9	4	1	7	3	5
7	3	4	2	5	6	9	8	1
5	1	9	3	8	7	6	2	4

44

1	6	2	7	5	4	3	9	8
4	3	8	6	2	9	7	1	5
7	9	5	3	8	1	2	4	6
6	7	1	9	3	8	4	5	2
9	2	4	1	6	5	8	3	7
8	5	3	4	7	2	1	6	9
5	4	7	8	9	3	6	2	1
2	1	6	5	4	7	9	8	3
3	8	9	2	1	6	5	7	4

45

4	2	5	3	7	6	1	8	9
9	1	7	8	4	5	2	6	3
6	3	8	2	1	9	5	7	4
1	4	3	6	2	7	9	5	8
2	5	9	4	8	3	7	1	6
8	7	6	9	5	1	4	3	2
7	8	4	1	3	2	6	9	5
5	9	2	7	6	8	3	4	1
3	6	1	5	9	4	8	2	7

46

4	6	5	1	3	8	9	7	2
7	1	9	2	6	4	8	3	5
8	2	3	9	7	5	4	1	6
1	5	8	3	4	2	6	9	7
2	9	6	8	5	7	1	4	3
3	7	4	6	9	1	2	5	8
6	3	1	5	2	9	7	8	4
9	4	2	7	8	3	5	6	1
5	8	7	4	1	6	3	2	9

47

2	5	9	8	7	3	6	1	4
7	1	6	5	4	9	2	8	3
8	4	3	1	2	6	5	9	7
6	3	7	9	1	8	4	2	5
5	8	4	7	6	2	9	3	1
1	9	2	4	3	5	7	6	8
3	7	5	6	9	1	8	4	2
4	6	1	2	8	7	3	5	9
9	2	8	3	5	4	1	7	6

48

8	5	4	1	9	6	7	3	2
7	2	6	5	4	3	1	8	9
9	3	1	7	8	2	5	6	4
6	4	9	8	2	7	3	5	1
1	7	3	6	5	4	9	2	8
2	8	5	3	1	9	6	4	7
4	6	8	9	3	1	2	7	5
5	1	7	2	6	8	4	9	3
3	9	2	4	7	5	8	1	6

49

2	3	7	8	9	5	1	6	4
1	9	6	4	7	2	3	5	8
8	4	5	1	3	6	9	7	2
3	5	2	7	4	8	6	9	1
9	6	8	2	5	1	4	3	7
7	1	4	9	6	3	2	8	5
4	8	9	3	2	7	5	1	6
6	7	3	5	1	4	8	2	9
5	2	1	6	8	9	7	4	3

50

1	8	9	6	4	2	5	3	7
6	7	4	5	3	8	2	9	1
2	3	5	1	7	9	6	4	8
5	6	8	9	1	7	4	2	3
7	4	2	3	5	6	8	1	9
3	9	1	8	2	4	7	5	6
4	1	3	7	8	5	9	6	2
9	2	7	4	6	3	1	8	5
8	5	6	2	9	1	3	7	4

51

7	5	3	1	4	9	8	6	2
1	9	6	5	8	2	7	3	4
8	4	2	7	6	3	9	5	1
9	1	4	3	2	8	6	7	5
2	3	5	6	1	7	4	8	9
6	7	8	9	5	4	2	1	3
5	2	9	8	7	1	3	4	6
4	6	7	2	3	5	1	9	8
3	8	1	4	9	6	5	2	7

52

5	9	7	3	6	4	1	2	8
1	6	3	2	9	8	7	5	4
2	4	8	1	7	5	3	9	6
7	8	9	4	5	2	6	1	3
3	1	6	7	8	9	2	4	5
4	2	5	6	1	3	8	7	9
9	7	2	8	4	6	5	3	1
6	5	1	9	3	7	4	8	2
8	3	4	5	2	1	9	6	7

53

9	7	3	6	1	5	8	2	4
2	4	8	7	3	9	1	5	6
1	6	5	4	8	2	3	9	7
4	3	9	2	6	7	5	1	8
5	8	7	1	9	4	6	3	2
6	2	1	3	5	8	7	4	9
3	1	2	8	4	6	9	7	5
8	9	4	5	7	3	2	6	1
7	5	6	9	2	1	4	8	3

54

9	2	7	8	3	1	5	4	6
8	4	6	7	2	5	3	9	1
3	5	1	4	6	9	2	7	8
1	8	9	5	4	7	6	3	2
4	3	2	9	8	6	7	1	5
7	6	5	3	1	2	4	8	9
5	9	4	2	7	8	1	6	3
2	1	3	6	9	4	8	5	7
6	7	8	1	5	3	9	2	4

55

8	5	2	9	4	6	3	7	1
7	1	6	3	5	2	4	8	9
9	4	3	7	1	8	2	5	6
6	9	1	2	7	4	5	3	8
5	8	4	6	3	1	9	2	7
2	3	7	8	9	5	6	1	4
4	2	8	1	6	3	7	9	5
3	7	5	4	8	9	1	6	2
1	6	9	5	2	7	8	4	3

56

4	5	6	8	7	2	3	9	1
1	8	2	3	4	9	5	6	7
7	3	9	1	6	5	8	2	4
2	7	4	5	3	6	1	8	9
8	9	5	2	1	7	6	4	3
3	6	1	4	9	8	2	7	5
6	1	3	9	8	4	7	5	2
5	4	7	6	2	3	9	1	8
9	2	8	7	5	1	4	3	6

57

5	2	4	3	7	9	1	8	6
7	1	6	8	2	5	9	3	4
8	3	9	4	1	6	7	2	5
9	5	2	6	3	4	8	1	7
1	4	8	7	9	2	5	6	3
6	7	3	1	5	8	4	9	2
4	8	1	5	6	3	2	7	9
3	9	7	2	4	1	6	5	8
2	6	5	9	8	7	3	4	1

58

3	4	5	9	6	1	8	7	2
6	2	7	3	5	8	4	1	9
1	8	9	2	4	7	5	6	3
9	7	8	4	3	6	2	5	1
4	1	2	8	7	5	3	9	6
5	6	3	1	2	9	7	4	8
8	3	6	7	1	4	9	2	5
7	9	1	5	8	2	6	3	4
2	5	4	6	9	3	1	8	7

59

1	9	8	5	6	2	4	3	7
6	7	3	1	4	9	5	8	2
2	4	5	3	7	8	6	9	1
4	3	1	9	5	6	7	2	8
8	5	7	2	1	3	9	6	4
9	2	6	7	8	4	3	1	5
3	1	9	4	2	5	8	7	6
5	8	2	6	3	7	1	4	9
7	6	4	8	9	1	2	5	3

60

3	9	1	4	6	5	2	7	8
8	7	4	1	3	2	6	9	5
5	6	2	7	8	9	3	1	4
2	5	6	8	4	1	7	3	9
9	3	8	6	5	7	1	4	2
1	4	7	2	9	3	8	5	6
7	2	5	9	1	8	4	6	3
6	1	3	5	2	4	9	8	7
4	8	9	3	7	6	5	2	1

Drastic Puzzle Solutions

Oh, no! Just as we're getting to the answers for the Drastic puzzles, out from the pages creeps an unwelcome visitor.

"Har har!" he says with an evil leer.

Argh! It's your arch enemy Professor Fiendish, and look — the diabolical villain has seized the remaining solutions! What ghastly plan can he have in mind?

"I bet you've just had a quick glance at the puzzles and given up, haven't you?" he cackles. "So now you're begging for the answers, aren't you!"

Well, really, of all the nerve. Of course you haven't given up and you certainly aren't begging for the answers. You're just . . . ahem . . . having a very quick glance through the solutions for research purposes. Besides, it's none of his business. There's only one thing to do. You sharpen your pencil and prepare to attack . . .

That should keep him quiet for a while.

61

2	6	7	3	9	4	8	5	1
1	8	3	6	5	2	9	4	7
9	4	5	1	7	8	2	6	3
8	3	9	7	1	5	6	2	4
5	7	2	4	6	3	1	8	9
4	1	6	2	8	9	7	3	5
3	2	8	9	4	1	5	7	6
7	5	1	8	3	6	4	9	2
6	9	4	5	2	7	3	1	8

62

6	5	1	7	3	8	2	4	9
2	4	9	5	1	6	8	3	7
7	3	8	9	2	4	5	6	1
1	6	2	3	4	7	9	8	5
4	8	5	6	9	2	1	7	3
9	7	3	8	5	1	6	2	4
5	9	4	2	8	3	7	1	6
3	2	6	1	7	9	4	5	8
8	1	7	4	6	5	3	9	2

63

1	2	6	9	5	7	8	4	3
9	8	4	2	3	1	7	5	6
5	7	3	8	4	6	1	9	2
8	4	9	7	2	3	6	1	5
7	5	1	6	8	4	3	2	9
6	3	2	1	9	5	4	8	7
2	1	7	5	6	8	9	3	4
3	9	8	4	7	2	5	6	1
4	6	5	3	1	9	2	7	8

64

8	5	3	6	2	7	1	4	9
1	4	9	5	3	8	7	2	6
2	7	6	4	1	9	3	5	8
7	8	5	3	4	1	6	9	2
6	1	2	9	7	5	8	3	4
3	9	4	2	8	6	5	7	1
5	3	1	8	9	4	2	6	7
9	6	7	1	5	2	4	8	3
4	2	8	7	6	3	9	1	5

65

8	5	2	6	7	9	3	4	1
6	1	4	2	3	8	9	5	7
3	9	7	4	1	5	2	8	6
1	8	9	7	2	6	4	3	5
7	4	6	5	9	3	1	2	8
2	3	5	8	4	1	7	6	9
5	2	1	3	6	7	8	9	4
4	7	8	9	5	2	6	1	3
9	6	3	1	8	4	5	7	2

66

1	9	3	7	2	4	5	6	8
5	7	8	1	6	3	2	9	4
6	2	4	5	8	9	1	7	3
4	3	5	8	9	7	6	1	2
7	6	1	3	5	2	8	4	9
9	8	2	4	1	6	3	5	7
3	1	6	9	7	8	4	2	5
2	4	9	6	3	5	7	8	1
8	5	7	2	4	1	9	3	6

67

5	6	1	7	3	9	8	2	4
8	9	3	2	1	4	5	6	7
7	4	2	5	8	6	9	3	1
4	5	8	6	7	2	1	9	3
6	1	9	3	4	8	7	5	2
3	2	7	9	5	1	4	8	6
1	3	5	8	2	7	6	4	9
9	8	4	1	6	3	2	7	5
2	7	6	4	9	5	3	1	8

68

4	2	8	1	3	7	6	5	9
6	9	7	5	2	8	4	3	1
5	3	1	4	6	9	8	7	2
2	8	3	7	9	5	1	6	4
9	7	4	8	1	6	3	2	5
1	5	6	3	4	2	7	9	8
3	4	9	6	5	1	2	8	7
7	1	2	9	8	3	5	4	6
8	6	5	2	7	4	9	1	3

69

5	4	6	2	8	9	3	7	1
2	8	7	3	6	1	5	4	9
1	9	3	5	4	7	2	8	6
9	1	4	6	7	5	8	3	2
3	2	8	9	1	4	7	6	5
6	7	5	8	2	3	1	9	4
8	6	1	7	9	2	4	5	3
7	5	2	4	3	6	9	1	8
4	3	9	1	5	8	6	2	7

70

3	6	9	2	4	8	5	7	1
1	4	8	7	5	6	9	2	3
5	7	2	1	9	3	6	8	4
9	1	4	5	2	7	8	3	6
2	8	3	6	1	4	7	5	9
7	5	6	3	8	9	1	4	2
6	2	1	4	7	5	3	9	8
8	3	5	9	6	2	4	1	7
4	9	7	8	3	1	2	6	5

71

9	3	6	2	5	4	1	7	8
8	2	5	7	1	9	4	6	3
7	4	1	3	6	8	9	2	5
1	6	3	4	8	2	5	9	7
4	8	7	5	9	1	6	3	2
5	9	2	6	3	7	8	4	1
6	7	4	8	2	5	3	1	9
2	1	8	9	4	3	7	5	6
3	5	9	1	7	6	2	8	4

72

6	4	9	1	2	5	3	7	8
8	3	7	9	6	4	2	5	1
5	2	1	8	7	3	4	6	9
4	5	3	7	9	6	8	1	2
9	7	8	5	1	2	6	3	4
1	6	2	3	4	8	7	9	5
3	1	4	6	8	9	5	2	7
2	9	5	4	3	7	1	8	6
7	8	6	2	5	1	9	4	3

73

6	3	2	7	1	5	9	8	4
5	4	8	2	9	6	3	7	1
7	1	9	4	8	3	6	5	2
2	6	5	3	4	9	8	1	7
1	7	3	8	5	2	4	6	9
9	8	4	1	6	7	2	3	5
8	2	6	5	7	4	1	9	3
4	9	7	6	3	1	5	2	8
3	5	1	9	2	8	7	4	6

74

6	7	1	8	4	3	9	5	2
9	3	5	1	7	2	6	8	4
4	8	2	5	9	6	1	3	7
1	5	9	6	2	8	4	7	3
3	6	8	4	5	7	2	9	1
7	2	4	3	1	9	5	6	8
5	1	7	9	3	4	8	2	6
8	4	3	2	6	5	7	1	9
2	9	6	7	8	1	3	4	5

75

7	2	9	3	1	8	4	6	5
5	8	1	7	4	6	3	9	2
4	6	3	9	5	2	1	8	7
6	7	4	1	8	5	2	3	9
3	1	8	4	2	9	7	5	6
2	9	5	6	3	7	8	1	4
9	3	6	2	7	1	5	4	8
1	5	2	8	6	4	9	7	3
8	4	7	5	9	3	6	2	1

76

1	2	4	5	8	3	9	6	7
8	7	6	2	9	4	5	3	1
3	9	5	6	7	1	4	2	8
7	3	9	4	1	2	8	5	6
6	8	2	9	5	7	1	4	3
4	5	1	3	6	8	7	9	2
2	1	3	7	4	5	6	8	9
5	6	7	8	3	9	2	1	4
9	4	8	1	2	6	3	7	5

77

6	2	8	5	1	4	3	7	9
1	9	7	3	6	2	8	5	4
4	3	5	8	9	7	1	2	6
8	7	6	1	3	5	4	9	2
3	4	9	7	2	6	5	8	1
5	1	2	4	8	9	7	6	3
9	5	4	6	7	3	2	1	8
2	8	3	9	5	1	6	4	7
7	6	1	2	4	8	9	3	5

78

1	6	2	5	4	3	8	7	9
3	5	7	9	6	8	4	1	2
4	8	9	1	7	2	3	6	5
5	9	6	7	3	1	2	4	8
7	4	8	6	2	5	1	9	3
2	1	3	8	9	4	6	5	7
9	2	4	3	5	6	7	8	1
8	3	5	4	1	7	9	2	6
6	7	1	2	8	9	5	3	4

79

5	1	8	2	4	7	3	9	6
7	4	9	6	3	1	2	5	8
2	6	3	8	5	9	7	4	1
4	8	5	1	2	6	9	3	7
9	7	1	4	8	3	6	2	5
3	2	6	7	9	5	1	8	4
1	9	2	5	7	8	4	6	3
6	5	4	3	1	2	8	7	9
8	3	7	9	6	4	5	1	2

80

4	3	6	7	1	9	5	2	8
5	9	1	2	4	8	6	3	7
8	7	2	6	5	3	4	1	9
2	4	9	1	7	5	8	6	3
1	5	7	3	8	6	9	4	2
6	8	3	9	2	4	1	7	5
7	2	5	8	6	1	3	9	4
3	6	4	5	9	2	7	8	1
9	1	8	4	3	7	2	5	6

81

4	7	1	6	5	9	3	8	2
6	2	8	3	7	1	5	9	4
5	9	3	2	4	8	7	6	1
1	8	6	9	3	4	2	5	7
7	3	5	8	1	2	6	4	9
2	4	9	7	6	5	1	3	8
3	6	4	1	8	7	9	2	5
9	5	7	4	2	6	8	1	3
8	1	2	5	9	3	4	7	6

82

6	1	9	8	5	4	7	2	3
4	5	7	6	3	2	8	9	1
8	2	3	7	9	1	4	5	6
3	8	2	1	4	6	9	7	5
7	9	5	2	8	3	6	1	4
1	6	4	5	7	9	2	3	8
5	7	1	9	6	8	3	4	2
2	3	6	4	1	7	5	8	9
9	4	8	3	2	5	1	6	7

83

1	9	8	7	2	6	3	5	4
6	3	2	4	8	5	1	9	7
4	5	7	9	1	3	8	6	2
9	7	3	5	4	8	6	2	1
2	6	1	3	9	7	4	8	5
5	8	4	2	6	1	9	7	3
8	1	5	6	3	2	7	4	9
3	2	9	8	7	4	5	1	6
7	4	6	1	5	9	2	3	8

84

4	7	8	6	9	1	3	5	2
1	6	9	2	5	3	8	7	4
2	3	5	4	8	7	6	1	9
3	4	7	9	6	2	5	8	1
6	8	1	5	3	4	9	2	7
5	9	2	1	7	8	4	3	6
8	1	4	3	2	6	7	9	5
9	2	3	7	4	5	1	6	8
7	5	6	8	1	9	2	4	3

85

5	1	6	4	9	3	7	2	8
9	8	2	6	5	7	1	3	4
3	4	7	1	8	2	6	5	9
4	9	3	5	1	8	2	6	7
7	2	1	3	6	4	8	9	5
8	6	5	2	7	9	4	1	3
2	7	4	9	3	1	5	8	6
6	3	8	7	2	5	9	4	1
1	5	9	8	4	6	3	7	2

86

6	8	3	9	7	1	5	2	4
5	7	2	4	3	6	1	8	9
4	1	9	5	8	2	7	6	3
2	3	4	7	6	9	8	1	5
8	5	7	1	4	3	6	9	2
9	6	1	2	5	8	4	3	7
1	4	8	3	2	7	9	5	6
7	2	6	8	9	5	3	4	1
3	9	5	6	1	4	2	7	8

87

6	4	3	1	7	9	5	8	2
9	8	5	3	2	6	7	4	1
2	1	7	8	4	5	3	9	6
7	9	4	2	5	1	6	3	8
5	3	2	6	8	4	1	7	9
1	6	8	7	9	3	2	5	4
4	7	6	9	3	2	8	1	5
3	2	9	5	1	8	4	6	7
8	5	1	4	6	7	9	2	3

88

1	8	9	7	4	6	2	5	3
2	3	4	9	5	1	8	6	7
5	7	6	3	8	2	9	4	1
7	2	1	6	9	4	3	8	5
3	9	5	8	1	7	4	2	6
4	6	8	2	3	5	1	7	9
6	1	7	4	2	9	5	3	8
8	5	2	1	7	3	6	9	4
9	4	3	5	6	8	7	1	2

89

6	3	7	4	2	8	9	1	5
4	8	1	7	5	9	3	2	6
9	5	2	1	3	6	4	8	7
5	7	9	8	4	3	2	6	1
8	2	6	9	1	5	7	4	3
3	1	4	6	7	2	5	9	8
7	6	5	2	9	1	8	3	4
2	4	8	3	6	7	1	5	9
1	9	3	5	8	4	6	7	2

90

8	4	1	3	2	9	6	7	5
6	2	7	8	5	4	9	1	3
3	9	5	6	1	7	8	2	4
7	8	4	1	6	2	5	3	9
9	1	3	5	4	8	7	6	2
5	6	2	9	7	3	4	8	1
4	7	9	2	8	1	3	5	6
1	3	6	7	9	5	2	4	8
2	5	8	4	3	6	1	9	7

Diabolical Puzzle Solutions

Phew, at last! Here are all the solutions to the hardest puzzles in the book. Did you think some of them were impossible? Not to worry, here they are all neatly laid out in order for you.

But just a minute, who's that in the distance? It's Professor Fiendish and he seems to be carrying something behind his back. Surely he wouldn't dare to bother us again? Besides, we've got all the solutions here, so what can he do?

Oh, no! He's sabotaged the rest of the book! All the solutions have been blown everywhere and . . . they are all in the wrong order!

How fiendish. Now if you want to find the solution to one of the Diabolical puzzles, you'll have to match up a few numbers from each puzzle to find the right answer.

DON'T FORGET THE DIABOLICAL SOLUTIONS HAVE BEEN MIXED UP!

11	2	13	7	19	17	23	5	3
3	7	19	23	5	2	13	11	17
23	5	17	11	3	13	7	19	2
17	23	11	13	7	5	3	2	19
19	3	7	2	11	23	5	17	13
2	13	5	3	17	19	11	23	7
5	19	23	17	13	3	2	7	11
13	11	2	19	23	7	17	3	5
7	17	3	5	2	11	19	13	23

4	6	7	5	1	2	9	8	3
5	1	8	4	3	9	6	2	7
3	2	9	8	7	6	4	1	5
9	4	5	3	6	8	2	7	1
1	7	2	9	5	4	3	6	8
8	3	6	7	2	1	5	4	9
7	9	4	2	8	3	1	5	6
6	5	3	1	4	7	8	9	2
2	8	1	6	9	5	7	3	4

4	6	1	9	5	2	8	7	3
5	8	7	3	1	6	2	4	9
3	2	9	4	8	7	6	5	1
1	3	6	8	7	9	4	2	5
9	4	2	6	3	5	7	1	8
7	5	8	2	4	1	3	9	6
2	9	5	7	6	3	1	8	4
6	1	4	5	2	8	9	3	7
8	7	3	1	9	4	5	6	2

9	2	4	7	8	5	3	6	1
6	3	1	4	9	2	8	7	5
7	8	5	3	1	6	2	9	4
5	9	7	2	4	8	1	3	6
3	1	6	5	7	9	4	2	8
8	4	2	6	3	1	9	5	7
4	6	8	9	5	3	7	1	2
2	7	3	1	6	4	5	8	9
1	5	9	8	2	7	6	4	3

7	2	4	1	9	5	8	3	6
5	8	6	4	7	3	2	1	9
3	9	1	6	2	8	5	4	7
2	7	3	9	6	1	4	8	5
9	4	8	7	5	2	3	6	1
1	6	5	3	8	4	9	7	2
6	1	2	8	4	9	7	5	3
4	5	7	2	3	6	1	9	8
8	3	9	5	1	7	6	2	4

6	8	4	7	1	3	2	9	5
9	2	3	6	8	5	7	4	1
7	5	1	9	4	2	6	3	8
2	1	6	4	3	9	8	5	7
3	9	8	5	2	7	1	6	4
4	7	5	1	6	8	3	2	9
1	6	7	2	5	4	9	8	3
5	3	9	8	7	6	4	1	2
8	4	2	3	9	1	5	7	6

2	9	1	5	6	7	4	8	3
8	4	6	9	2	3	1	7	5
5	7	3	8	1	4	2	9	6
9	6	4	3	5	8	7	2	1
7	1	2	4	9	6	3	5	8
3	5	8	2	7	1	6	4	9
1	8	5	7	3	2	9	6	4
6	2	9	1	4	5	8	3	7
4	3	7	6	8	9	5	1	2

3	7	5	4	9	2	8	1	6
6	8	2	5	7	1	3	9	4
1	4	9	8	3	6	2	5	7
8	9	6	2	5	3	4	7	1
7	1	4	9	6	8	5	3	2
2	5	3	7	1	4	6	8	9
9	2	8	1	4	5	7	6	3
4	6	7	3	8	9	1	2	5
5	3	1	6	2	7	9	4	8

5	4	7	1	3	9	6	2	8
8	2	6	7	5	4	9	1	3
1	9	3	6	8	2	5	7	4
9	6	2	8	4	1	3	5	7
3	5	4	2	6	7	8	9	1
7	1	8	5	9	3	4	6	2
6	3	1	9	2	8	7	4	5
4	7	5	3	1	6	2	8	9
2	8	9	4	7	5	1	3	6

6	4	9	7	8	3	2	1	5
3	7	2	5	1	4	9	8	6
5	8	1	6	2	9	7	3	4
9	6	3	1	4	5	8	7	2
2	1	7	9	6	8	5	4	3
4	5	8	3	7	2	1	6	9
7	2	4	8	5	6	3	9	1
8	9	5	4	3	1	6	2	7
1	3	6	2	9	7	4	5	8

In the end . . .

City: Chicago, Illinois
Place: Lou's Diner, Upper Main St.
Date: October 2, 1928
Time: 10:01 pm

The door of Lou's Diner flew open and slammed back against the wall as Blade Bolton and his associates barged their way inside.

"Where's Dolly?" gasped Blade.

"Oh, mama," muttered Lou from behind the counter. He was staring in horror at the door.

"You're one minute late, Blade," said a voice which seemed to come through the mail slot.

Slowly the door swung away from the wall revealing a rather squashed-looking Dolly Snowlips.

"She was just hanging her coat up behind the door when you guys showed up," explained Lou as he ducked for safety behind his counter.

Very slowly the seven men tried to back out of the doorway again, but they just succeeded in getting stuck. Dolly stepped out to face them. In her hands was a square cardboard box which, knowing Dolly, could have contained a bomb or a snake or a set of incriminating photographs. Whatever it was, they didn't want to know.

"Look, Dolly," pleaded Blade. "Sorry about the door and everything, but we did it! We did the Sookoodooyookoo thing. We've spent all day on it!"

R	A	S	8	C	T	D	U	3
D	T	8	A	U	3	C	S	R
3	C	U	D	S	R	8	A	T
A	8	R	C	3	D	S	T	U
C	S	3	R	T	U	A	D	8
T	U	D	S	8	A	R	3	C
8	3	C	T	A	S	U	R	D
U	D	A	3	R	8	T	C	S
S	R	T	U	D	C	3	8	A

Sure enough, Blade was holding out a completed grid. To his astonishment Dolly smiled.

"I guess I over-reacted in the park," she said. "After all, you dopes gave everybody such a laugh this morning. If you guys were in the slammer, we'd have nothing to brighten our day. So to make it up to you I made you all a cake."

Dolly put the box on the table. They all groaned. A cake made by Dolly was probably as scary as anything else she might have had in the box.

"Hey!" said Dolly, offended. "My cooking ain't so bad. People are *still* talking about my stuffed turkey dinner."

Behind the counter Lou nodded to himself. People were still talking about Dolly's stuffed turkey, and no wonder. Dolly hadn't realized that you don't stuff a turkey with the same stuff that you'd stuff a cushion with. But then again, you didn't go telling Dolly things like that, at least not if you wanted your diner to have any windows left.

"We're sure it's a lovely cake," said Blade. "It's just that, what with doing this crossword number thing, we've seen enough squares for today."

The others muttered in agreement, mightily relieved that Blade had thought of a good excuse not to eat the cake.

"Yeah," agreed Porky. "Although your cakes are really lovely, we couldn't bear the thought of a square-shaped one."

"Then relax, boys!" smiled Dolly. "I've got a lovely surprise for you!"